D1442038

HOW-TO LIBRARY

MAKING JEWELRY WITH RUBBER BANDS

Written and Illustrated by Kathleen Petelinsek

CHERRY LAKE PUBLISHING • ANN ARBOR, MICHIGAN

CHERRY
LAKE
Publishing

Published in the United States of America by Cherry Lake Publishing
Ann Arbor, Michigan
www.cherrylakepublishing.com

Pages 4 and 5, ©mervas/Shutterstock.com; page 29, ©Monkey Business Images/Shutterstock.com.

Library of Congress Cataloging-in-Publication Data
Petelinsek, Kathleen, author.
  Making jewelry with rubber bands / by Kathleen Petelinsek.
     pages cm. — (Crafts) (How-to library)
  Includes bibliographical references and index.
  Summary: "Learn how to create a variety of fun craft projects using colorful rubber bands and looms" — Provided by publisher.
  Audience: Grades 4 to 6.
  ISBN 978-1-63137-781-5 (lib. bdg.) — ISBN 978-1-63137-801-0 (pbk.) — ISBN 978-1-63137-841-6 (e-book) — ISBN 978-1-63137-821-8 (pdf)
  1. Jewelry making—Juvenile literature. 2. Handicraft—Juvenile literature. 3. Costume jewelry—Juvenile literature. 4. Rubber bands—Juvenile literature. 5. Bracelets—Juvenile literature. 6. Handlooms—Juvenile literature. I. Title.

  TT212.P4812 2014
  745.5942—dc23   2014003984

Cherry Lake Publishing would like to acknowledge the work of The Partnership for 21st Century Skills. Please visit *www.p21.org* for more information.

Printed in the United States of America
Corporate Graphics Inc.
July 2014

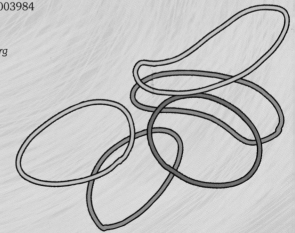

TABLE OF CONTENTS

Who Invented Rubber Band Jewelry?

Rubber band jewelry is a lot of fun to make and share with friends.

You have probably seen some of your classmates wearing jewelry made from colorful rubber bands. Rubber band jewelry is one of the fastest-growing craft trends today. How did it all get started?

A Malaysian **immigrant** named Cheong Choon Ng became interested as he watched his two daughters make crafts by wrapping small rubber bands together. Ng's fingers were too large to wrap the rubber bands like his girls could, so in 2010, he invented a **loom** to help hold the bands. Ng called his invention Twistz Bandz. It was a wooden board made with pushpins and hooks, and it was a huge hit with the Ng family. Ng decided to **manufacture** and sell the boards to other rubber band crafters. He had the parts shipped to his Michigan home, and his entire family assembled the looms there. Ng renamed his product the Rainbow Loom. His niece and nephew came up with the new name.

Ng's early efforts to sell the Rainbow Loom were unsuccessful. People didn't understand how to use it. Then he built a Web site featuring instructional videos hosted by his daughters and niece. The site was a success! Ng received his first order for the Rainbow Loom in the summer of 2012, and demand for the product began to grow. By August 2013, popular craft stores across the United States were stocking Ng's invention. More than 1.2 million of the Rainbow Loom have been sold so far!

It is easy to learn how to make jewelry using the Rainbow Loom.

Tools and Materials

You do not need many supplies to begin crafting with rubber bands. You will be able to find everything you need at a local craft store. Here is a list:

- **Loom:** There are several brands of looms available. In addition to the Rainbow Loom, many stores carry the FunLoom and the Cra-Z-Loom.

- **Rubber bands:** Rubber bands should be ½ inch (1.3 cm) to ¾ inch (2 cm) in **diameter**. They come in a wide variety of colors. You can buy them in bags with assorted colors or as individual colors.

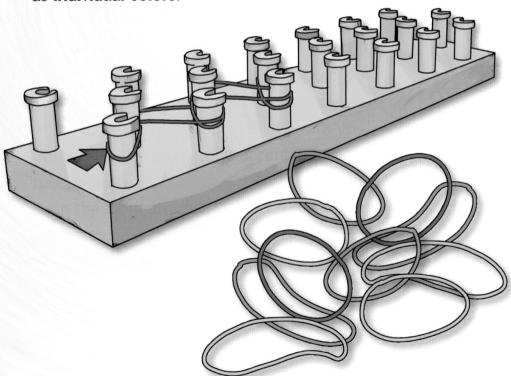

- **Small crochet hook:** You will need a small **crochet hook** to work with your loom. You can also make some items without the loom, using just the crochet hook. The hook should be size G, 4.25 millimeters.
- **Plastic C clips:** These clips come with most looms and rubber band packages. You can also buy them separately.
- **Beads:** You will need beads to create some of the projects in this book. Plastic beads with large holes in the center work the best. You can buy large containers of plastic beads in an assortment of colors and shapes.
- **Plastic compartment case:** It is easier to keep your supplies sorted if you use a case with individual dividers in it. You can sort rubber bands and beads by color and keep all of your plastic clips together.

You can purchase your loom and other supplies together as a kit. Many loom kits have everything you need to get started, including the loom, rubber bands, a crochet hook, and small plastic clips.

Basic Chain Bracelets

Chain using a Hook

Not all rubber band jewelry projects require a loom. This simple bracelet is made using only rubber bands and a crochet hook.

Materials
- Crochet hook
- Rubber bands (at least 25, any colors)

Steps

1. Hold your crochet hook in one hand. Wrap one rubber band around the hooked end two times. Push the wrapped rubber band about ½ inch (1.3 cm) down toward the non-hooked end.

2. Hook a second band onto the crochet hook. Hold the rubber band from step 1 in place. Pull the second rubber band through the center of the wrapped band. Turn the crochet hook toward you and slide the wrapped band off the crochet hook and into the center of the second rubber band.

3. Now loop the end of the second rubber band back onto the hook. The first rubber band will be underneath the hook.

4. Continue to repeat steps 2 and 3 until your chain is as long as you want it to be.

5. To finish your chain, create a slipknot. Remove the crochet hook, but keep the previous stitch centered on the two loops of the final rubber band. Now pull one of the loops of the final rubber band through the other and pull it tight.

Chain Using a Loom

This bracelet is made using a process very similar to the one you used in the previous activity. However, this one uses the loom. It is good to practice this bracelet so you can learn how the crochet hook works together with the loom.

Materials

- Loom
- 25 rubber bands
- Crochet hook
- Plastic C clip

Steps

1. Position your loom so the arrow is at the bottom, facing away from you. Your loom will face this direction when you begin almost every project.
2. Place the first rubber band around the center peg closest to you and stretch it to the bottom right peg.

Always start loading your rubber bands at the arrow.

3. If you would like a bracelet with alternating colors, use the second color for your next rubber band. Place the second rubber band on the peg you stretched the previous band to. Stretch the second band back toward the center column of the loom. Wrap it around the peg one above from where you began the first band.

4. Place a third band on the peg you just ended on and stretch it to the right. Wrap it around the peg one above the one you wrapped your second band around in the right column.

5. Continue this zigzag pattern until all the pegs in the center and the right column have rubber bands around them. Always remember to start your rubber band on the peg you just ended on, stretching it to the right or left to create the zigzag.

6. Once your loom is loaded, turn it around so the arrow is at the top, facing you.

7. Start in the center peg closest to you. Push your crochet hook down into the center of the peg. Hook the bottom rubber band with your hook and pull it up off the peg, making sure

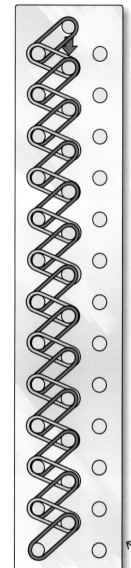

Once your loom is loaded, turn it around so the arrow is at the top.

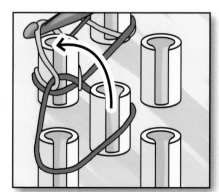

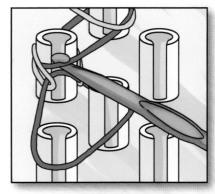

the top rubber band stays on the peg. Stretch the hooked rubber band left, back to the other peg it is looped on. This is called looping a band back to the peg it came from.

8. Now push the hook down into the peg that you just looped the rubber band around and grab the bottom band. Pull it off the peg and loop it back to the peg it came from.

9. Continue looping the bands back to the pegs they came from, one at a time in order.

10. Now hook a plastic C clip around both strands of the last rubber band you looped back. This is the rubber band that is on the center peg by the red arrow.

11. While holding the clip, gently tug the rubber bands off the loom one by one.

12. Attach the last rubber band to come off the loom to the plastic clip to create a bracelet.

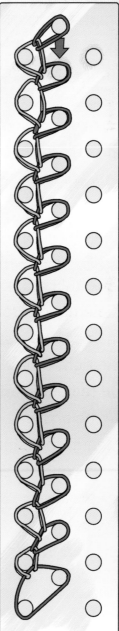

Loading the Loom and Other Tips

Now that you have created your first bracelets and you have a feel for the tools, it is time to learn a few helpful tips.

Loom tips: Filling your loom in a pattern of rubber bands is called loading the loom. The patterns are diagrammed using colors and numbers. Load the loom using the illustrated band color, starting with band number 1. If the pattern requires a bead, it will show this as well. Many of the crafts in this book will start with a loom diagram so you can begin by loading your loom. The steps after you have loaded the loom will tell you how to hook the bands together. On the right is an example of a pattern for the bracelet you just made on pages 9–11.

   Remember to always load your loom starting with the arrow at the bottom of the loom, facing away from you. If you start loading it the other way, you will not be able to unhook your rubber bands.

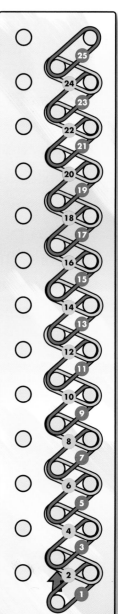

When loading the loom with multiple layers of rubber bands, make certain to push the first layer all the way down the pegs. You need to be able to see the order of each layer on each peg as you work. Load each layer carefully so that the middle layer is in the middle of the peg and the top layer is at the top of the peg.

Crochet hook tips: As you may have noticed while working on your first loom project, it can be easy to hook the wrong rubber band. To avoid this, always push your crochet needle through the peg with the hook facing the red arrow on the loom. This keeps you from accidentally grabbing the wrong band. As you pull the band off the peg, you can turn the crochet hook slightly to pull it where it needs to go.

Basic Bead Bracelet

This project will give you an opportunity to work with beads. Try different types of beads to create a wide variety of bracelet styles.

Materials

- Loom
- 25 rubber bands (12 of one color and 13 of the other color)
- 25 beads
- Crochet hook
- Plastic C clip

Steps

1. Load the loom according to the diagram. To add a bead, thread the rubber band through the hole in the bead first, and then stretch the ends of the rubber band onto the loom.
2. Once your loom is loaded, turn the loom around so the arrow is at the top, facing you.

Load your loom like this. Remember to turn the loom around before hooking the bands.

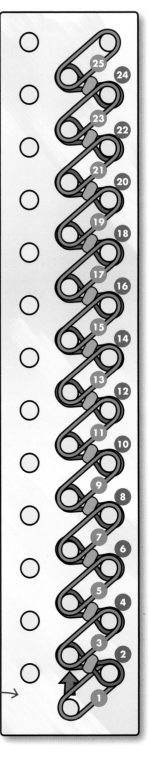

3. Now you are ready to start hooking the rubber bands together. Start looping bands back to the peg they came from one at a time, just as you did for the basic loom bracelet on pages 9–11. Begin with the rubber band closest to you with a bead on it.

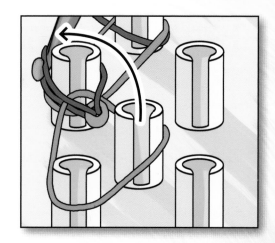

4. When you reach the end, hook a plastic clip around both strands of the last rubber band you looped back.

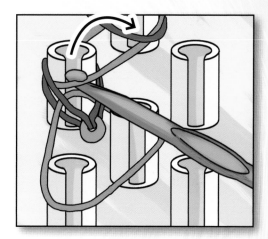

5. Hold on to the clip and gently tug the rubber bands off the loom.

6. Attach the last rubber band to come off the loom to the plastic C clip to create a bracelet.

Fishtail Bracelet

This simple bracelet requires only two pegs on your loom, but the pattern it creates is quite complex. Try alternating colors every other or every third band to create different styles.

Materials

- Loom
- 50 rubber bands
- Crochet hook
- Plastic C clip

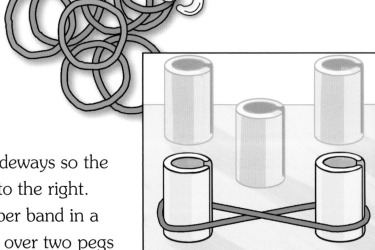

Steps

1. Turn your loom sideways so the arrow is pointing to the right.
2. Place the first rubber band in a figure eight shape over two pegs that are next to each other. This is the only band that you will twist into a figure eight.
3. Place two more rubber bands over the same two pegs. Do not twist the bands this time. If you want alternating colors, use a different color for the first of the two bands you place.

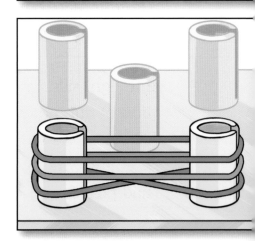

4. Use your crochet hook to grab the rubber band on the bottom of the left peg and hook it up and off the peg it was on, letting it move to the center of the two remaining bands. Do not put your hook in the center of the peg. Instead, grab the band from the side to pull it up and over.

5. Do the same with the right side, looping it up and off the peg and letting it slide onto the two remaining rubber bands.

6. Add another band to the two pegs. Be sure to keep your color pattern in mind.

7. Use your crochet hook to grab the left side of the bottom rubber band and hook it up and off the peg it was on. Do the same with the right side. Like before, do not put the hook in the center of the peg, but rather grab the band from the side and pull it over.

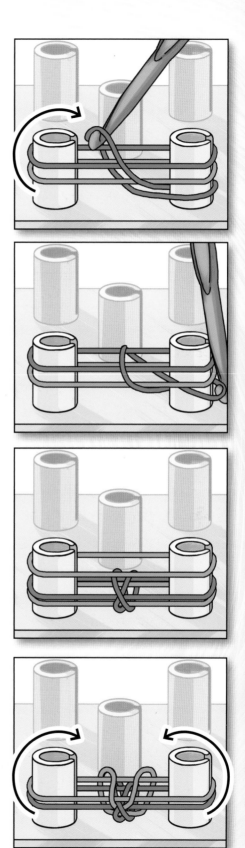

8. Add another rubber band to the two pegs again and keep repeating until you are out of rubber bands.

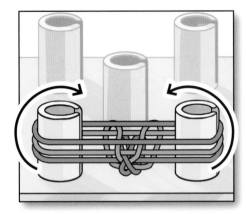

9. When you are out of rubber bands, add a clip to the last rubber band that you unhooked from the pegs. Make sure you hook both sides of the rubber band with the clip.

10. Now unhook the two bands that are still on pegs. These rubber bands will slide out of your bracelet. They are not needed, so set them aside.

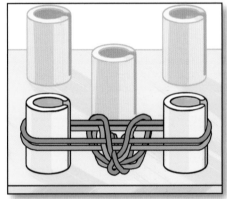

11. To make a bracelet, bring the clip around to the end of the bracelet with no hook and attach the ends together.

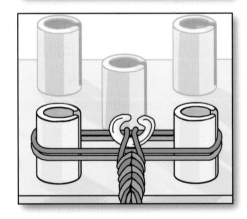

Fishtail Ring

Create an entire jewelry set by making a ring and earrings (*see page 21*) to match your fishtail bracelet (*see pages 16–18*).

Materials

- Loom
- 20 rubber bands
- Crochet hook
- 1 bead
- Plastic C clip

Steps

1. Begin just as you did when you created the fishtail bracelet. Turn your loom sideways. The arrow should be pointing to the right. Follow steps 2 through 8 on pages 16–18 until you have used nine rubber bands.

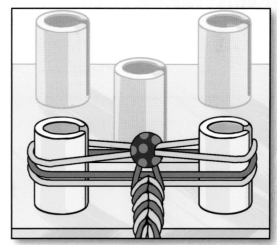

2. Add a bead to the 10th rubber band before placing it on the loom.

3. Now continue adding rubber bands (following steps 2 through 8 on pages 16–18) until you have used all 20.

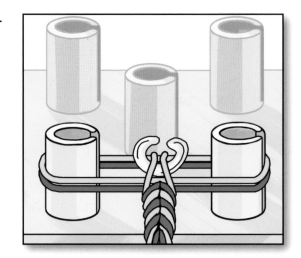

4. When you are out of rubber bands, add a clip to the last rubber band that you unhooked from the pegs. Make sure you hook both sides of the rubber band with the clip.

5. Now unhook the two bands that are still on pegs. These rubber bands will slide out of your ring. They are not needed, so set them aside.

6. Bring the clip around to the end of the ring with no hook and attach the ends together.

Fishtail Earrings

Materials

- Loom
- 42 rubber bands (divided into two groups of 20—one group for each earring—plus two more that will be discarded when the project is complete)
- Crochet hook
- 2 French hook earring wires

Steps

1. Follow steps 1 through 3 on pages 19–20 for making a ring, alternating band colors if you wish. Do not add the bead on the 10th rubber band, though.
2. When you have used 20 rubber bands and you have just two bands left on the pegs, loop the bottom band off the pegs as you did the other rubber bands.
3. Loop the last band back to one side and create a slipknot with it.
4. Remove the fishtail from the loom and loop the rubber band with the slipknot in it back through the other end of the fishtail to form a loop.
5. Thread the looped band onto a French hook earring wire.
6. Make a second earring so you have one for each ear.

Triple Stitch Bracelet

Make a bracelet using your favorite team colors.

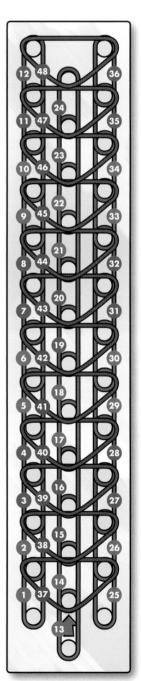

Materials

- Loom
- 18 rubber bands (first team color)
- 18 rubber bands (second team color)
- 13 rubber bands (accent color)
- Crochet hook
- Plastic C clip

Steps

1. Load the loom according to the diagram. You can use any team colors. In this case, we have used blue and red. Our accent color is dark gray. Make sure the loom is loaded with the arrow at the bottom, facing away from you. You should use all but one accent colored rubber band.
2. Turn the loom around so the arrow is on top, facing you.
3. Starting at the bottom left, grab the bottom team color band, loop it up through the gray accent color band, and hook it to the peg above it in the column. If you do not loop it through

the accent color band as shown, the bracelet will not stay together.

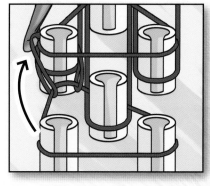

4. Loop the entire left column the same way, Make sure to pull each band up through the accent band.

5. Now move to the center column. Start with the band that is closest to you. Loop it back to where each is hooked. Loop the entire center column back.

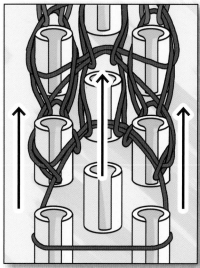

6. Loop the right column the same way. Again, make sure that you pull each band up through the accent color and not around it.

7. At the very top of the loom, move the two rubber band loops that are on the top left peg to the center peg. Do the same with the rubber bands on the right. You should now have six loops around the top center peg.

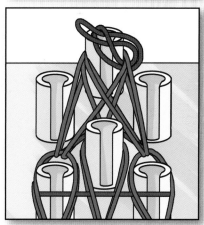

8. Carefully thread the remaining accent color band through the six loops. Make a slipknot around all six loops.

9. Hold on to the slipknot and gently pull the bands from your loom. Add a clip to each side of the single bands at the ends of the bracelet.

Candy Cane Charm

These charms can be used to decorate your other rubber band creations. You can make two of them to create earrings. Hang a charm from one of your rubber band chains to make a necklace. You could even use one to decorate a wrapped gift.

Materials

- Loom
- 13 white rubber bands
- 13 red rubber bands
- Crochet hook

Steps

1. Make sure your loom is facing the right direction. Load it according to the diagram. This diagram is a bit different from previous ones because we are using triple bands in some places. The triple bands give the candy cane thickness.
2. Wrap the 13th red rubber band around the last peg four times.
3. Rotate the loom so the arrow is on the top side and facing toward you.

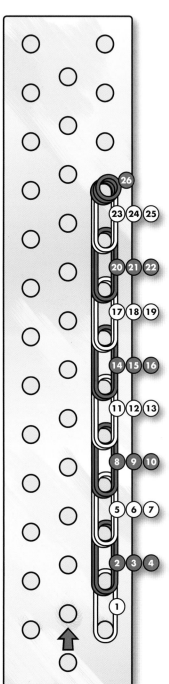

4. Poke your crochet hook all the way to the bottom of the peg that has the last rubber band wrapped three times around it. Hook the three white rubber bands and pull them up over the peg and onto the peg they came from.

5. Poke your crochet hook into the peg where you just added the white bands. Pull the red rubber bands up and around, hooking them back to the peg they came from. This is the basic looping pattern we learned on pages 9–11, only using three rubber bands at a time.

6. Continue hooking until you have hooked the last three bands back to the peg they came from.

7. On the last single rubber band, make a slipknot and pull it tight. Remove the rubber bands from the loom by gently pulling you creation from the slipknot. They should form a thick, straight candy cane.

8. Now poke your needle through the fourth stitch down from the slipknot and grab the slipknot using your crochet hook. Pull it through the cane. This will curl the top of your cane and create a loop to hang your cand cane from.

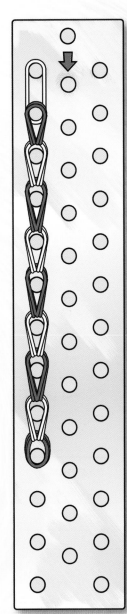

Flower Necklace

This necklace is made up of colorful flower charms. We will start by making the flowers. Then we will string the flowers together using a basic chain.

Materials

Flower

- Loom
- 6 orange rubber bands (outside center color)
- 7 yellow rubber bands (center color)
- 6 red rubber bands (petal color)
- Crochet hook

Chain

- Rubber bands (number and color depend on how long you want your chain to be and what color you want)
- Crochet hook
- Plastic C clip

Steps

1. Make sure your loom is facing the right direction. Load your loom according to the three diagrams at the top of page 27. Each diagram represents a layer. Begin with diagram 1. Band 19 (the 7th yellow rubber band) should be double wrapped around the center peg as shown in diagram 3.

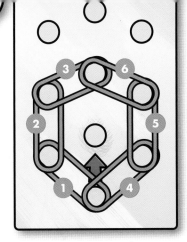

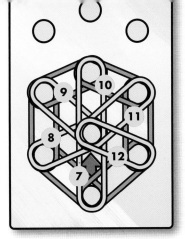

Diagram 1　　　　　Diagram 2　　　　　Diagram 3

2. Turn the loom around so that the arrow is at the top and facing you. Poke your crochet hook into the center peg and grab the top yellow band underneath the double wrapped rubber band in the center. Loop it back to the peg it came from.

3. Continue around the flower counterclockwise, looping each band from the center back to the peg it came from.

4. After you are finished looping the entire flower, make sure the loom has the arrow at the top, facing you. Push your hook down into the bottom center peg and hook the second to the bottom orange rubber band. Pull it up and to the left to hook it back onto the hook it came from.

5. Loop the two other orange bands on the left side of the **hexagon**.

6. Go back to the bottom center peg and grab the bottom orange rubber band. Loop it right, onto the peg it came from.

Step 4 starts here with the arrow on the loom facing you.

7. Loop the remaining two rubber bands on the right back to the loops they came from.
8. Put your crochet hook down through the top center peg. Holding one end of a chain rubber band, hook the other end to the crochet hook in the top center peg. Pull the rubber band up through all the rubber bands on that peg and make a slipknot.
9. Gently pull the flower from the loom.
10. Put a second chain color rubber band through the slipknot. This band should double hook around your crochet hook. Your crochet hook is now in place to make the chain. Follow the instructions for the basic hook chain on pages 8–9. Make the chain as long as you want it to be. End the chain with a plastic clip.
11. Loop the chain back around near the flower and clip it into a link at the beginning.

Ideas Galore!

As you have looped and hooked your way through the crafts in this book, you may have come up with some ideas of your own. Draw them in a sketchbook as they come to you. This will help you organize, plan, and further develop your ideas. You can also sketch diagrams for loom patterns to share with your friends.

Ask an adult to help you search the Internet for more rubber band jewelry ideas.

Another great resource for ideas is the Internet. There are many videos online. Always be careful when searching for ideas online. Ask an adult to help you. As you search the Internet, can you think of things to make projects different from what is online? Sketch your ideas into your sketchbook and make the idea your own.

Glossary

crochet hook (kroh-SHAY HOOK) a hooked needle that is used to loop together stitches of thread to make a cloth item

diameter (dye-AM-i-tur) a straight line through the center of a circle, connecting opposite sides

hexagon (HEK-suh-gahn) a shape with six straight sides

immigrant (IM-i-gruhnt) someone who moves from one country to another and settles there

loom (LOOM) a machine or device for weaving cloth or other objects

manufacture (man-yuh-FAK-chur) to make something, often with machines

For More Information

Books

Dorsey, Colleen. *Totally Awesome Rubber Band Jewelry.* East Petersburg, PA: Design Originals, 2013.

McCann, John, and Becky Thomas. *Loom Magic!* New York: Sky Pony Press, 2013.

Peterson, Suzanne M. *The Loomatic's Interactive Guide to the Rainbow Loom.* Reno, NV: Hijinx, LLC, 2013.

Web Sites

Funtastic Ideas

http://funtasticideas.com

Rubber bands aren't just for bracelets. Visit this site for videos showing how to make insects, people, even musical instruments!

Rainbow Loom—Instructional Videos

www.rainbowloom.com/instructions

Check out the Rainbow Loom Web site for instructions on how to make tons of different bracelets.

Index

About the Author

Kathleen Petelinsek is a children's book illustrator, writer, and designer. As a child, she spent her summers drawing and painting. She still loves to do the same today, but now all her work is done on the computer. When she isn't working on her computer, she can be found outside swimming, biking, running, or playing in the snow of southern Minnesota.